2022

# WILD FLOWERS
# PLANNER

*by*
*Sze Wing Vetault*

# This planner belongs to:

# Also by Sze Wing Vetault

## Books and Other Products

Goddess with Many Faces

21 Days of Inspiration

Goddess Weekly Planner

Goddess Daily Planner

Spring Bloom Journal

For more information and free resources, please visit:
www.SzeWingVetault.com

*When the path reveals itself,*

*follow it.*

*- Cheryl Strayed*

*When a woman decides to be herself and only herself,*
*she lives from the wisdom of her heart and acts from*
*the love of her soul. She transcends and transforms*
*the power from the outer world to the inner realm.*

*- Sze Wing Vetualt*

Thank you so much for starting your year with me!

This Wild Flowers Planner is more than just a tool to plan your year ahead. It is a companion to help you to set goals and review them periodically. You will also find moon phases and dates to remind you of the lunar cycles while you plan your weeks and months.

A part of uncovering your feminine wisdom is being able to follow your energy ebb and flow. There are some days in a month where you may feel more creative, productive or energetic. On the other hand, there are times you may need extra rest or a quiet time to reflect. Ideas sprout when we allow time and space for our minds to empty.

This planner is designed to help you to plan your work, play and rest more effectively. By regularly using this planner, you will naturally become more aware of your body's rhythms and emotional needs.

May you embark on a great year ahead with this planner!

With love,

Sze Wing Vetault

# 2022

## January

| M | T | W | T | F | S | S |
|---|---|---|---|---|---|---|
|  |  |  |  |  | 1 | 2 |
| 3 | 4 | 5 | 6 | 7 | 8 | 9 |
| 10 | 11 | 12 | 13 | 14 | 15 | 16 |
| 17 | 18 | 19 | 20 | 21 | 22 | 23 |
| 24 | 25 | 26 | 27 | 28 | 29 | 30 |
| 31 |  |  |  |  |  |  |

●:3  ◗:10  ○:18  ◖:26

## February

| M | T | W | T | F | S | S |
|---|---|---|---|---|---|---|
|  | 1 | 2 | 3 | 4 | 5 | 6 |
| 7 | 8 | 9 | 10 | 11 | 12 | 13 |
| 14 | 15 | 16 | 17 | 18 | 19 | 20 |
| 21 | 22 | 23 | 24 | 25 | 26 | 27 |
| 28 |  |  |  |  |  |  |

●:1  ◗:9  ○:17  ◖:24

## March

| M | T | W | T | F | S | S |
|---|---|---|---|---|---|---|
|  | 1 | 2 | 3 | 4 | 5 | 6 |
| 7 | 8 | 9 | 10 | 11 | 12 | 13 |
| 14 | 15 | 16 | 17 | 18 | 19 | 20 |
| 21 | 22 | 23 | 24 | 25 | 26 | 27 |
| 28 | 29 | 30 | 31 |  |  |  |

●:3  ◗:10  ○:18  ◖:25

## April

| M | T | W | T | F | S | S |
|---|---|---|---|---|---|---|
|  |  |  |  | 1 | 2 | 3 |
| 4 | 5 | 6 | 7 | 8 | 9 | 10 |
| 11 | 12 | 13 | 14 | **15** | 16 | 17 |
| **18** | 19 | 20 | 21 | 22 | 23 | 24 |
| 25 | 26 | 27 | 28 | 29 | 30 |  |

●:1  ◗:9  ○:17  ◖:23

## May

| M | T | W | T | F | S | S |
|---|---|---|---|---|---|---|
|  |  |  |  |  |  | 1 |
| 2 | 3 | 4 | 5 | 6 | 7 | 8 |
| 9 | 10 | 11 | 12 | 13 | 14 | 15 |
| 16 | 17 | 18 | 19 | 20 | 21 | 22 |
| 23 | 24 | 25 | 26 | 27 | 28 | 29 |
| 30 | 31 |  |  |  |  |  |

◗:1  ◗:9  ○:16  ◖:23  ●:30

## June

| M | T | W | T | F | S | S |
|---|---|---|---|---|---|---|
|  |  | 1 | 2 | 3 | 4 | 5 |
| 6 | 7 | 8 | 9 | 10 | 11 | 12 |
| 13 | 14 | 15 | 16 | 17 | 18 | 19 |
| 20 | 21 | 22 | 23 | 24 | 25 | 26 |
| 27 | 28 | 29 | 30 |  |  |  |

◗:8  ○:14  ◖:21  ●:29

## July

| M | T | W | T | F | S | S |
|---|---|---|---|---|---|---|
|  |  |  |  | 1 | 2 | 3 |
| 4 | 5 | 6 | 7 | 8 | 9 | 10 |
| 11 | 12 | 13 | 14 | 15 | 16 | 17 |
| 18 | 19 | 20 | 21 | 22 | 23 | 24 |
| 25 | 26 | 27 | 28 | 29 | 30 | 31 |

◗:7  ○:14  ◖:21  ●:29

## August

| M | T | W | T | F | S | S |
|---|---|---|---|---|---|---|
| 1 | 2 | 3 | 4 | 5 | 6 | 7 |
| 8 | 9 | 10 | 11 | 12 | 13 | 14 |
| 15 | 16 | 17 | 18 | 19 | 20 | 21 |
| 22 | 23 | 24 | 25 | 26 | 27 | 28 |
| 29 | 30 | 31 |  |  |  |  |

◗:5  ○:12  ◖:19  ●:27

## September

| M | T | W | T | F | S | S |
|---|---|---|---|---|---|---|
|  |  |  | 1 | 2 | 3 | 4 |
| 5 | 6 | 7 | 8 | 9 | 10 | 11 |
| 12 | 13 | 14 | 15 | 16 | 17 | 18 |
| 19 | 20 | 21 | 22 | 23 | 24 | 25 |
| 26 | 27 | 28 | 29 | 30 |  |  |

◗:4  ○:10  ◖:18  ●:26

## October

| M | T | W | T | F | S | S |
|---|---|---|---|---|---|---|
|  |  |  |  |  | 1 | 2 |
| 3 | 4 | 5 | 6 | 7 | 8 | 9 |
| 10 | 11 | 12 | 13 | 14 | 15 | 16 |
| 17 | 18 | 19 | 20 | 21 | 22 | 23 |
| 24 | 25 | 26 | 27 | 28 | 29 | 30 |
| 31 |  |  |  |  |  |  |

◗:3  ○:10  ◖:18  ●:25

## November

| M | T | W | T | F | S | S |
|---|---|---|---|---|---|---|
|  | 1 | 2 | 3 | 4 | 5 | 6 |
| 7 | 8 | 9 | 10 | 11 | 12 | 13 |
| 14 | 15 | 16 | 17 | 18 | 19 | 20 |
| 21 | 22 | 23 | 24 | 25 | 26 | 27 |
| 28 | 29 | 30 |  |  |  |  |

◗:1  ○:8  ◖:17  ●:24

## December

| M | T | W | T | F | S | S |
|---|---|---|---|---|---|---|
|  |  |  | 1 | 2 | 3 | 4 |
| 5 | 6 | 7 | 8 | 9 | 10 | 11 |
| 12 | 13 | 14 | 15 | 16 | 17 | 18 |
| 19 | 20 | 21 | 22 | 23 | 24 | **25** |
| **26** | 27 | 28 | 29 | 30 | 31 |  |

◗:1  ○:8  ◖:16  ●:23  ◗:30

---

**21 Mar** ● Harmony Day
**21 Mar** ● March Equinox
**15 Apr** ● Good Friday
**17 Apr** ● Easter Sunday (All)
**18 Apr** ● Easter Monday

**21 Jun** ● June Solstice
**23 Sep** ● September Equinox
**15 Oct** ● International Pregnancy and Infant Loss Remembrance Day
**11 Nov** ● Remembrance Day

**22 Dec** ● December Solstice
**24 Dec** ● Christmas Eve
**25 Dec** ● Christmas Day
**26 Dec** ● Boxing Day
**31 Dec** ● New Year's Eve

# Year Plan

| JANUARY | FEBRUARY | MARCH |
|---|---|---|
| APRIL | MAY | JUNE |
| JULY | AUGUST | SEPTEMBER |
| OCTOBER | NOVEMBER | DECEMBER |

New Year
New Goals

# Year Review

## WHAT DID I ACCOMPLISH?

## WHAT WERE MY SET BACKS?

# Year Review

WHAT DID I LEARN?

WHAT DO I WANT TO CHANGE?

# New Year Goals

MY TOP 10 GOALS

# New Year Goals

MY NEW YEAR PLANS

# Moon Dates

## 2022

# Moon Phases

**New Moon:** It's time to make a fresh start, set new intentions, sow new seeds, initiate new projects. Just keep it easy and light while the energy is still new.

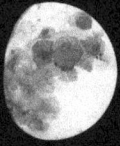

**Waxing Moon:** The moon is growing larger, energy is rising and expanding. It's a good time for brainstorming, planning and taking actions. Perfect for creating momentum or trying something new.

**Full Moon:** The moon is full in the sky, energy is peaking and it's time to be seen or heard. Great time to make an announcement, launch or pitch a project/product and connect or celebrate with others.

**Waning Moon:** The moon is growing smaller in the sky. Energy is reducing and signaling a time to finish up loose ends and complete the work you have in hand.

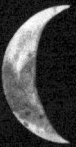

**Balsamic Moon:** "Balsamic" means healing and soothing. As the moon continues to grow smaller, it's time to make peace with where you are and appreciate all the blessings in your life. Trust in divine timing.

**Dark Moon:** This is the day before new moon begins. It's a good time to rest and reflect. You may feel you need a bath or go to bed early. Slow down and relax.

|  | Northern Hemisphere | | Southern Hemisphere | |
|---|---|---|---|---|
|  | New Moon | Full Moon | New Moon | Full Moon |
| January | 2 | 17 | 3 | 18 |
| February | 1 | 16 | 1 | 17 |
| March | 2 | 18 | 3 | 18 |
| April | 1 & 30 | 16 | 1 | 17 |
| May | 30 | 16 | 1 & 30 | 16 |
| June | 28 | 14 | 29 | 14 |
| July | 28 | 13 | 29 | 14 |
| August | 27 | 11 | 27 | 12 |
| September | 25 | 10 | 26 | 10 |
| October | 25 | 9 | 25 | 10 |
| November | 23 | 8 | 24 | 8 |
| December | 23 | 7 | 23 | 6 |

*Please Note: The moon phases in the monthly & weekly calendar are based on Southern Hemisphere dates. Please adjust accordingly.*

Tell me,
what is it you plan to do with
your one wild and precious life?

-Mary Oliver

# January

**KEY FOCUS FOR THIS MONTH:**

| MON | TUE | WED | THUR | FRI | SAT | SUN |
|-----|-----|-----|------|-----|-----|-----|
|     |     |     |      |     | 1   | 2   |
| 3 ● ♑ | 4 | 5 | 6 | 7 | 8 | 9 |
| 10  | 11  | 12  | 13   | 14  | 15  | 16  |
| 17  | 18 ☾ ♋ | 19 | 20 | 21 | 22 | 23 |
| 24  | 25  | 26  | 27   | 28  | 29  | 30  |

♑ NEW MOON IN CAPRICON    ♋ FULL MOON IN CANCER

# GOALS THIS MONTH:

# Weekly Planner

MOON PHASE:  NEW MOON / WAXING / FULL MOON / WANING

GOALS THIS WEEK:

REMINDER:

TO-DO LIST:

# Weekly Schedule

## December - January

27
MON
.......................................................................

28
TUE
.......................................................................

29
WED
.......................................................................

30
THURS
.......................................................................

31
FRI
.......................................................................

1
SAT
.......................................................................

2
SUN
.......................................................................

# Weekly Planner

MOON PHASE:   NEW MOON / WAXING / FULL MOON / WANING

GOALS THIS WEEK:

REMINDER:

TO-DO LIST:

# Weekly Schedule

## January

**3**
MON ●
............................................................

**4**
TUE
............................................................

**5**
WED
............................................................

**6**
THURS
............................................................

**7**
FRI
............................................................

**8**
SAT
............................................................

**9**
SUN
............................................................

# Weekly Planner

**MOON PHASE:** NEW MOON / WAXING / FULL MOON / WANING

GOALS THIS WEEK:

REMINDER:

TO-DO LIST:

# Weekly Schedule

## January

10
MON

........................................................................................

11
TUE

........................................................................................

12
WED

........................................................................................

13
THURS

........................................................................................

14
FRI

........................................................................................

15
SAT

........................................................................................

16
SUN

........................................................................................

# Weekly Planner

MOON PHASE:  NEW MOON / WAXING / FULL MOON / WANING

GOALS THIS WEEK:

REMINDER:

TO-DO LIST:

# Weekly Schedule

## January

17
MON

....................................................................................

18
TUE

....................................................................................

19
WED

....................................................................................

20
THURS

....................................................................................

21
FRI

....................................................................................

22
SAT

....................................................................................

23
SUN

....................................................................................

# Weekly Planner

MOON PHASE:  NEW MOON / WAXING / FULL MOON / WANING

GOALS THIS WEEK:

REMINDER:

TO-DO LIST:

# Weekly Schedule

## January

24
MON
..................................................................................................

25
TUE
..................................................................................................

26
WED
..................................................................................................

27
THURS
..................................................................................................

28
FRI
..................................................................................................

29
SAT
..................................................................................................

30
SUN
..................................................................................................

# February

KEY FOCUS FOR THIS MONTH:

| MON | TUE | WED | THUR | FRI | SAT | SUN |
|-----|-----|-----|------|-----|-----|-----|
| 31 | 1 ●〰 | 2 | 3 | 4 | 5 | 6 |
| 7 | 8 | 9 | 10 | 11 | 12 | 13 |
| 14 | 15 | 16 | 17 🌑♌ | 18 | 19 | 20 |
| 21 | 22 | 23 | 24 | 25 | 26 | 27 |
| 28 | | | | | | |

〰 New moon in Aquarius  ♌ Full moon in Leo

# GOALS THIS MONTH:

# Weekly Planner

MOON PHASE:  NEW MOON / WAXING / FULL MOON / WANING

GOALS THIS WEEK:

REMINDER:

TO-DO LIST:

# Weekly Schedule

## January - February

**31**
MON

.....................................................................................

**1** ●
TUE

.....................................................................................

**2**
WED

.....................................................................................

**3**
THURS

.....................................................................................

**4**
FRI

.....................................................................................

**5**
SAT

.....................................................................................

**6**
SUN

.....................................................................................

# Weekly Planner

**MOON PHASE:**  NEW MOON / WAXING / FULL MOON / WANING

### GOALS THIS WEEK:

### REMINDER:

### TO-DO LIST:

# Weekly Schedule

## February

**7**
MON
.....................................................................................

**8**
TUE
.....................................................................................

**9**
WED
.....................................................................................

**10**
THURS
.....................................................................................

**11**
FRI
.....................................................................................

**12**
SAT
.....................................................................................

**13**
SUN
.....................................................................................

# Weekly Planner

MOON PHASE:  NEW MOON / WAXING / FULL MOON / WANING

## GOALS THIS WEEK:

## REMINDER:

## TO-DO LIST:

# Weekly Schedule

## February

**14**
MON

..............................................................................

**15**
TUE

..............................................................................

**16**
WED

..............................................................................

**17**
THURS

..............................................................................

**18**
FRI

..............................................................................

**19**
SAT

..............................................................................

**20**
SUN

..............................................................................

# Weekly Planner

GOALS THIS WEEK:

REMINDER:

TO-DO LIST:

# Weekly Schedule

## February

21
MON
.......................................................................................

22
TUE
.......................................................................................

23
WED
.......................................................................................

24
THURS
.......................................................................................

25
FRI
.......................................................................................

26
SAT
.......................................................................................

27
SUN
.......................................................................................

# March

KEY FOCUS FOR THIS MONTH:

| MON | TUE | WED | THUR | FRI | SAT | SUN |
|-----|-----|-----|------|-----|-----|-----|
| 28 | 1 | 2 | 3 ● ♓ | 4 | 5 | 6 |
| 7 | 8 | 9 | 10 | 11 | 12 | 13 |
| 14 | 15 | 16 | 17 | 18 🌑 ♍ 19 | | 20 |
| 21 | 22 | 23 | 24 | 25 | 26 | 27 |
| 28 | 29 | 30 | 31 | | | |

♓ NEW MOON IN PISCES     ♍ FULL MOON IN VIRGO

## GOALS THIS MONTH:

# Weekly Planner

MOON PHASE: NEW MOON / WAXING / FULL MOON / WANING

GOALS THIS WEEK:

REMINDER:

TO-DO LIST:

# Weekly Schedule

## February - March

**28**
Mon

....................................................................................

**1**
Tue

....................................................................................

**2**
Wed

....................................................................................

**3** ●
Thurs

....................................................................................

**4**
Fri

....................................................................................

**5**
Sat

....................................................................................

**6**
Sun

....................................................................................

# Weekly Planner

MOON PHASE:  NEW MOON / WAXING / FULL MOON / WANING

GOALS THIS WEEK:

REMINDER:

TO-DO LIST:

# Weekly Schedule

## March

7
MON
....................................................................................

8
TUE
....................................................................................

9
WED
....................................................................................

10
THURS
....................................................................................

11
FRI
....................................................................................

12
SAT
....................................................................................

13
SUN

....................................................................................

# Weekly Planner

MOON PHASE:  NEW MOON / WAXING / FULL MOON / WANING

GOALS THIS WEEK:

REMINDER:

TO-DO LIST:

# Weekly Schedule

## March

14
MON

..................................................................................

15
TUE

..................................................................................

16
WED

..................................................................................

17
THURS

..................................................................................

18
FRI

..................................................................................

19
SAT

..................................................................................

20
SUN

..................................................................................

# Weekly Planner

### GOALS THIS WEEK:

### REMINDER:

### TO-DO LIST:

# Weekly Schedule

## March

21
MON

.............................................................................................

22
TUE

.............................................................................................

23
WED

.............................................................................................

24
THURS

.............................................................................................

25
FRI

.............................................................................................

26
SAT

.............................................................................................

27
SUN

.............................................................................................

# Weekly Planner

MOON PHASE:  NEW MOON / WAXING / FULL MOON / WANING

GOALS THIS WEEK:

REMINDER:

TO-DO LIST:

# Weekly Schedule

**March - April**

28
MON

.................................................................................

29
TUE

.................................................................................

30
WED

.................................................................................

31
THURS

.................................................................................

1 ●
FRI

.................................................................................

2
SAT

.................................................................................

3
SUN

.................................................................................

# Seasonal

# Review

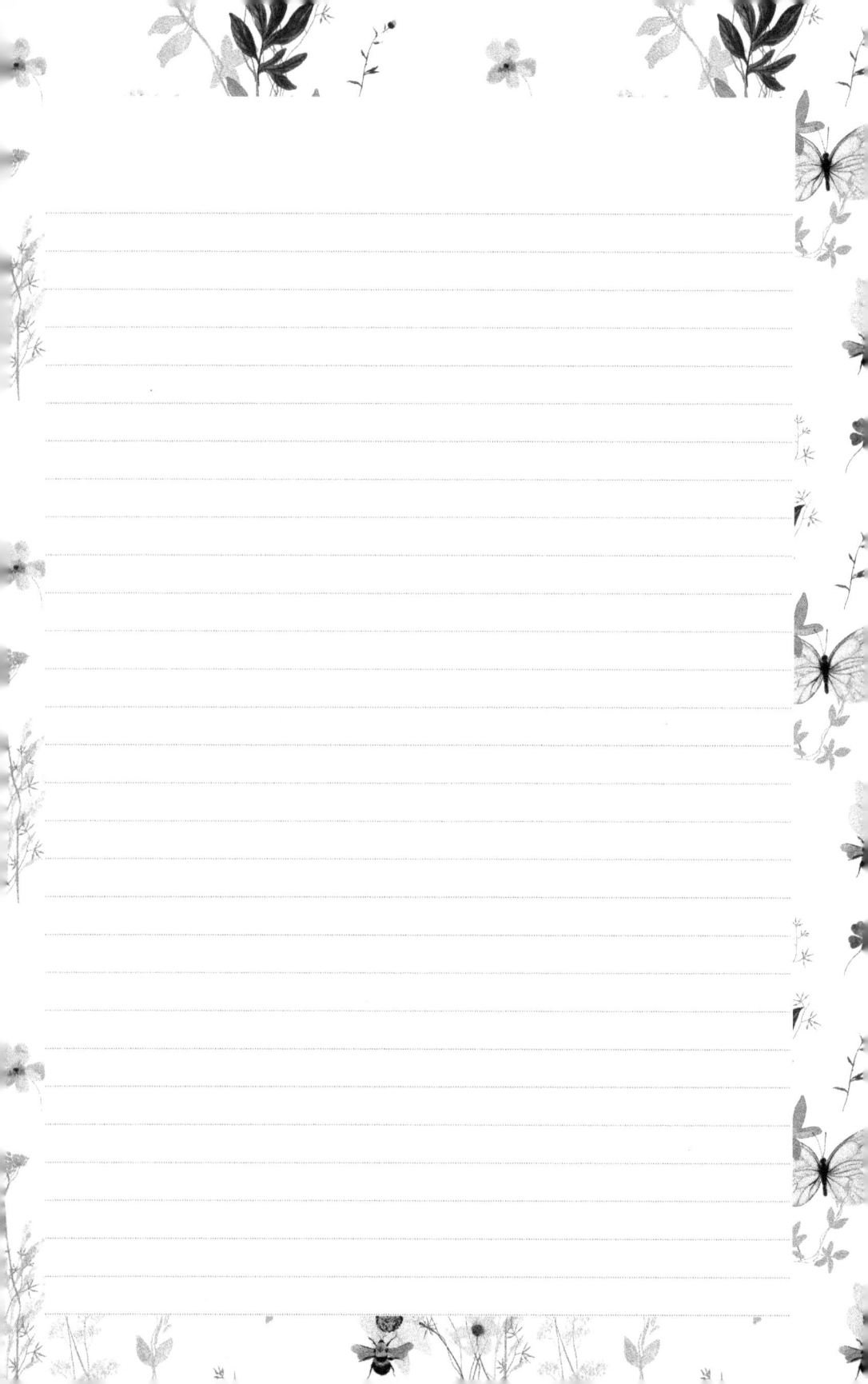

# April

**KEY FOCUS FOR THIS MONTH:**

| MON | TUE | WED | THUR | FRI | SAT | SUN |
|-----|-----|-----|------|-----|-----|-----|
| | | | | 1 ● ♈ | 2 | 3 |
| 4 | 5 | 6 | 7 | 8 | 9 | 10 |
| 11 | 12 | 13 | 14 | 15 | 16 | 17 ♎ |
| 18 | 19 | 20 | 21 | 22 | 23 | 24 |
| 25 | 26 | 27 | 28 | 29 | 30 | |

♈ NEW MOON IN ARIES    ♎ FULL MOON IN LIBRA

# GOALS THIS MONTH:

# Weekly Planner

MOON PHASE:  NEW MOON / WAXING / FULL MOON / WANING

### GOALS THIS WEEK:

### REMINDER:

### TO-DO LIST:

# Weekly Schedule

## April

**4**
MON

.......................................................................................................

**5**
TUE

.......................................................................................................

**6**
WED

.......................................................................................................

**7**
THURS

.......................................................................................................

**8**
FRI

.......................................................................................................

**9**
SAT

.......................................................................................................

**10**
SUN

.......................................................................................................

# Weekly Planner

**MOON PHASE:** NEW MOON / WAXING / FULL MOON / WANING

**GOALS THIS WEEK:**

**REMINDER:**

**TO-DO LIST:**

# Weekly Schedule

## April

11
MON

-------------------------------------------------

12
TUE

-------------------------------------------------

13
WED

-------------------------------------------------

14
THURS

-------------------------------------------------

15
FRI

-------------------------------------------------

16
SAT

-------------------------------------------------

17
SUN

-------------------------------------------------

# Weekly Planner

**MOON PHASE:** NEW MOON / WAXING / FULL MOON / WANING

### GOALS THIS WEEK:

### REMINDER:

### TO-DO LIST:

# Weekly Schedule

## April

**18**
MON

................................................................

**19**
TUE

................................................................

**20**
WED

................................................................

**21**
THURS

................................................................

**22**
FRI

................................................................

**23**
SAT

................................................................

**24**
SUN

................................................................

# Weekly Planner

**MOON PHASE:** NEW MOON / WAXING / FULL MOON / WANING

### GOALS THIS WEEK:

### REMINDER:

### TO-DO LIST:

# Weekly Schedule

25
MON
..........................................................................................

26
TUE
..........................................................................................

27
WED
..........................................................................................

28
THURS
..........................................................................................

29
FRI
..........................................................................................

30
SAT
..........................................................................................

1 ●
SUN
..........................................................................................

# May

**KEY FOCUS FOR THIS MONTH:**

| MON | TUE | WED | THUR | FRI | SAT | SUN |
|-----|-----|-----|------|-----|-----|-----|
|  |  |  |  |  |  | 1 ● ♉ |
| 2 | 3 | 4 | 5 | 6 | 7 | 8 |
| 9 | 10 | 11 | 12 | 13 | 14 | 15 |
| 16 ♏ | 17 | 18 | 19 | 20 | 21 | 22 |
| 23 | 24 | 25 | 26 | 27 | 28 | 29 |

♉ NEW MOON ECLIPSE IN TAURUS    ♏ FULL MOON ECLIPSE IN SCORPIO

GOALS THIS MONTH:

# Weekly Planner

MOON PHASE:   NEW MOON / WAXING / FULL MOON / WANING

GOALS THIS WEEK:

REMINDER:

TO-DO LIST:

# Weekly Schedule

## May

2
MON
...............................................................

3
TUE
...............................................................

4
WED
...............................................................

5
THURS
...............................................................

6
FRI

...............................................................

7
SAT
...............................................................

8
SUN
...............................................................

# Weekly Planner

MOON PHASE:  NEW MOON / WAXING / FULL MOON / WANING

GOALS THIS WEEK:

REMINDER:

TO-DO LIST:

# Weekly Schedule

## May

**9**
MON

.......................................................................................

**10**
TUE

.......................................................................................

**11**
WED

.......................................................................................

**12**
THURS

.......................................................................................

**13**
FRI

.......................................................................................

**14**
SAT

.......................................................................................

**15**
SUN

.......................................................................................

# Weekly Planner

GOALS THIS WEEK:

REMINDER:

TO-DO LIST:

# Weekly Schedule

## May

16
MON

.........................................................................

17
TUE

.........................................................................

18
WED

.........................................................................

19
THURS

.........................................................................

20
FRI

.........................................................................

21
SAT

.........................................................................

22
SUN

.........................................................................

# Weekly Planner

GOALS THIS WEEK:

REMINDER:

TO-DO LIST:

# Weekly Schedule

## May

23
MON

........................................................................................

24
TUE

........................................................................................

25
WED

........................................................................................

26
THURS

........................................................................................

27
FRI

........................................................................................

28
SAT

........................................................................................

29
SUN

........................................................................................

# June

**KEY FOCUS FOR THIS MONTH:**

| MON | TUE | WED | THUR | FRI | SAT | SUN |
|---|---|---|---|---|---|---|
| 30 ● ♊ 31 | | 1 | 2 | 3 | 4 | 5 |
| 6 | 7 | 8 | 9 | 10 | 11 | 12 |
| 13 | 14 🌑 ♐ 15 | | 16 | 17 | 18 | 19 |
| 20 | 21 | 22 | 23 | 24 | 25 | 26 |
| 27 | 28 | 29 ● ♋ 30 | | | | |

♊ New moon in Gemini     ♐ Super Full moon in Sagittarius

♋ New moon in Cancer

## GOALS THIS MONTH:

# Weekly Planner

MOON PHASE:  NEW MOON / WAXING / FULL MOON / WANING

GOALS THIS WEEK:

REMINDER:

TO-DO LIST:

# Weekly Schedule

## May - June

30 ●
MON

....................................................................................

31
TUE

....................................................................................

1
WED

....................................................................................

2
THURS

....................................................................................

3
FRI

....................................................................................

4
SAT

....................................................................................

5
SUN

....................................................................................

# Weekly Planner

MOON PHASE:  NEW MOON / WAXING / FULL MOON / WANING

GOALS THIS WEEK:

REMINDER:

TO-DO LIST:

# Weekly Schedule

## June

6
MON

7
TUE

8
WED

9
THURS

10
FRI

11
SAT

12
SUN

# Weekly Planner

MOON PHASE:  NEW MOON / WAXING / FULL MOON / WANING

GOALS THIS WEEK:

REMINDER:

TO-DO LIST:

# Weekly Schedule

## June

13
MON

..................................................................................................

14
TUE

..................................................................................................

15
WED

..................................................................................................

16
THURS

..................................................................................................

17
FRI

..................................................................................................

18
SAT

..................................................................................................

19
SUN

..................................................................................................

# Weekly Planner

MOON PHASE:  NEW MOON / WAXING / FULL MOON / WANING

GOALS THIS WEEK:

REMINDER:

TO-DO LIST:

# Weekly Schedule

## June

**20**
MON
..................................................................................

**21**
TUE
..................................................................................

**22**
WED
..................................................................................

**23**
THURS
..................................................................................

**24**
FRI
..................................................................................

**25**
SAT
..................................................................................

**26**
SUN
..................................................................................

# Weekly Planner

MOON PHASE:  NEW MOON / WAXING / FULL MOON / WANING

GOALS THIS WEEK:

REMINDER:

TO-DO LIST:

# Weekly Schedule

## June - July

27
MON

28
TUE

29 ●
WED

30
THURS

1
FRI

2
SAT

3
SUN

# Seasonal
# Review

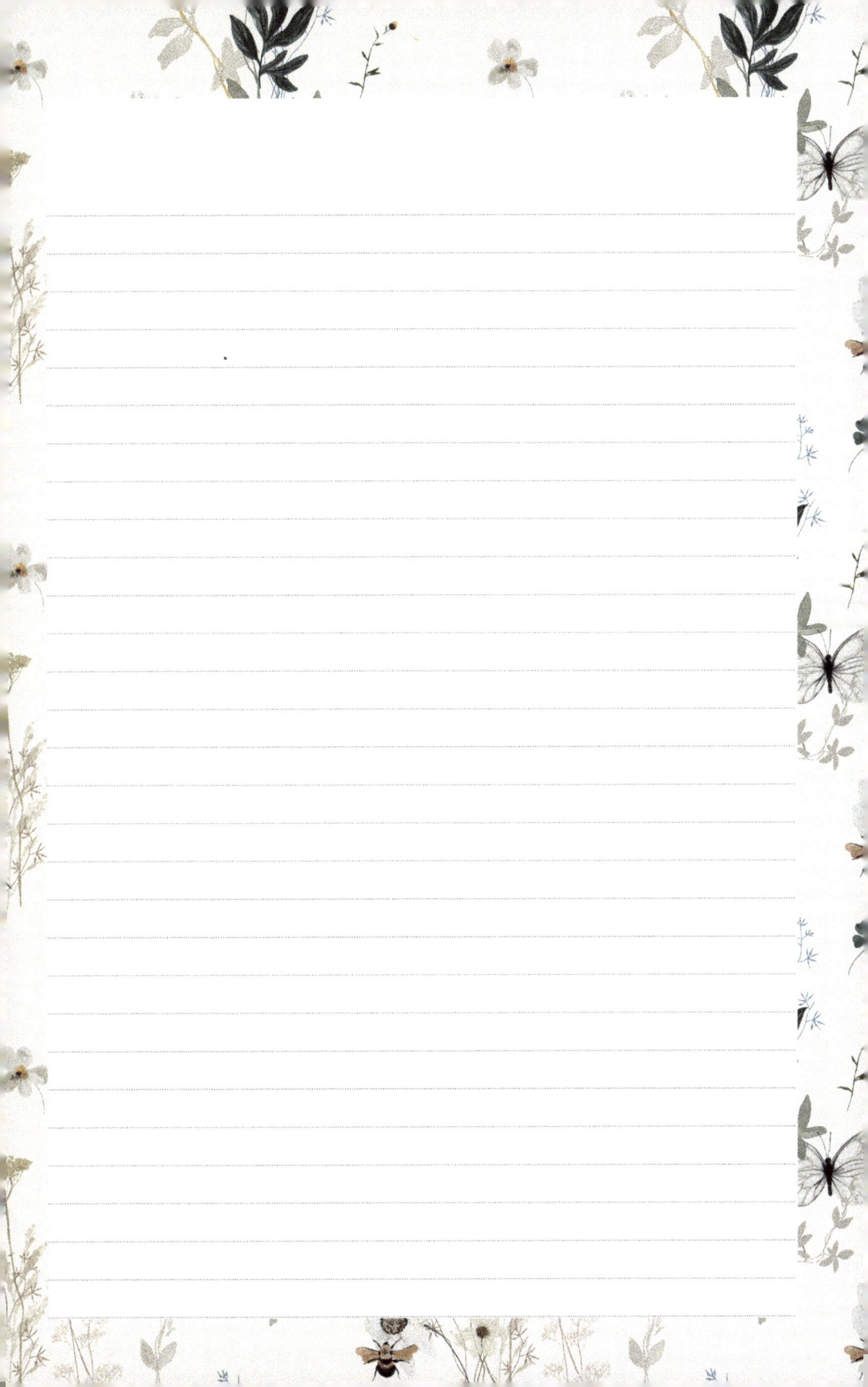

# July

### KEY FOCUS FOR THIS MONTH:

| MON | TUE | WED | THUR | FRI | SAT | SUN |
|---|---|---|---|---|---|---|
| | | | | 1 | 2 | 3 |
| 4 | 5 | 6 | 7 | 8 | 9 | 10 |
| 11 | 12 | 13 | 14 🌕 ♑ 15 | | 16 | 17 |
| 18 | 19 | 20 | 21 | 22 | 23 | 24 |
| 25 | 26 | 27 | 28 | 29 ● ♌ 30 | | 31 |

♑ SUPER FULL MOON IN CAPRICORN  ♌ NEW MOON IN LEO

# GOALS THIS MONTH:

# Weekly Planner

MOON PHASE:  NEW MOON / WAXING / FULL MOON / WANING

GOALS THIS WEEK:

REMINDER:

TO-DO LIST:

# Weekly Schedule

## July

**4**
MON
....................................................................................

**5**
TUE
....................................................................................

**6**
WED
....................................................................................

**7**
THURS
....................................................................................

**8**
FRI
....................................................................................

**9**
SAT
....................................................................................

**10**
SUN
....................................................................................

# Weekly Planner

MOON PHASE:  NEW MOON / WAXING / FULL MOON / WANING

GOALS THIS WEEK:

REMINDER:

TO-DO LIST:

# Weekly Schedule

## July

11
MON

12
TUE

13
WED

14
THURS

15
FRI

16
SAT

17
SUN

# Weekly Planner

MOON PHASE:  NEW MOON / WAXING / FULL MOON / WANING

GOALS THIS WEEK:

REMINDER:

TO-DO LIST:

# Weekly Schedule

## July

**18**
MON

....................................................................................................................

**19**
TUE

....................................................................................................................

**20**
WED

....................................................................................................................

**21**
THURS

....................................................................................................................

**22**
FRI

....................................................................................................................

**23**
SAT

....................................................................................................................

**24**
SUN

....................................................................................................................

# Weekly Planner

MOON PHASE:  NEW MOON / WAXING / FULL MOON / WANING

GOALS THIS WEEK:

REMINDER:

TO-DO LIST:

# Weekly Schedule

## July

### 25
MON

......................................................................

### 26
TUE

......................................................................

### 27
WED

......................................................................

### 28
THURS

......................................................................

### 29 ●
FRI

......................................................................

### 30
SAT

......................................................................

### 31
SUN

......................................................................

# August

KEY FOCUS FOR THIS MONTH:

| MON | TUE | WED | THUR | FRI | SAT | SUN |
|-----|-----|-----|------|-----|-----|-----|
| 1 | 2 | 3 | 4 | 5 | 6 | 7 |
| 8 | 9 | 10 | 11 | 12 ︴ 13 | | 14 |
| 15 | 16 | 17 | 18 | 19 | 20 | 21 |
| 22 | 23 | 24 | 25 | 26 | 27 ● ♍ 28 | |
| 29 | 30 | 31 | | | | |

︴ FULL MOON IN AQUARIUS   ♍ NEW MOON IN VIRGO

# GOALS THIS MONTH:

# Weekly Planner

MOON PHASE:  NEW MOON / WAXING / FULL MOON / WANING

GOALS THIS WEEK:

REMINDER:

TO-DO LIST:

# Weekly Schedule

## August

1

MON

................................................................

2

TUE

................................................................

3

WED

................................................................

4

THURS

................................................................

5

FRI

................................................................

6

SAT

................................................................

7

SUN

................................................................

# Weekly Planner

MOON PHASE:  NEW MOON / WAXING / FULL MOON / WANING

GOALS THIS WEEK:

REMINDER:

TO-DO LIST:

# Weekly Schedule

## August

**8**
MON
...........................................................................................

**9**
TUE
...........................................................................................

**10**
WED
...........................................................................................

**11**
THURS
...........................................................................................

**12**
FRI
...........................................................................................

**13**
SAT
...........................................................................................

**14**
SUN
...........................................................................................

# Weekly Planner

**MOON PHASE:  NEW MOON / WAXING / FULL MOON / WANING**

## GOALS THIS WEEK:

## REMINDER:

## TO-DO LIST:

# Weekly Schedule

## August

| | |
|---|---|
| 15 MON | |
| 16 TUE | |
| 17 WED | |
| 18 THURS | |
| 19 FRI | |
| 20 SAT | |
| 21 SUN | |

# Weekly Planner

MOON PHASE: NEW MOON / WAXING / FULL MOON / WANING

GOALS THIS WEEK:

REMINDER:

TO-DO LIST:

# Weekly Schedule

## August

22
MON

---

23
TUE

---

24
WED

---

25
THURS

---

26
FRI

---

27 ●
SAT

---

28
SUN

---

# September

KEY FOCUS FOR THIS MONTH:

| MON | TUE | WED | THUR | FRI | SAT | SUN |
|-----|-----|-----|------|-----|-----|-----|
|     |     |     | 1 | 2 | 3 | 4 |
| 5 | 6 | 7 | 8 | 9 | 10 ♓ | 11 |
| 12 | 13 | 14 | 15 | 16 | 17 | 18 |
| 19 | 20 | 21 | 22 | 23 | 24 | 25 |
| 26 ● ♎ | 27 | 28 | 29 | 30 |     |     |

♓ FULL MOON IN PISCES    ♎ NEW MOON IN LIBRA

# GOALS THIS MONTH:

# Weekly Planner

MOON PHASE:  NEW MOON / WAXING / FULL MOON / WANING

GOALS THIS WEEK:

REMINDER:

TO-DO LIST:

# Weekly Schedule

## August - September

29
MON
.....................................................................................................

30
TUE
.....................................................................................................

31
WED
.....................................................................................................

1
THURS
.....................................................................................................

2
FRI
.....................................................................................................

3
SAT
.....................................................................................................

4
SUN

.....................................................................................................

# Weekly Planner

MOON PHASE:  NEW MOON / WAXING / FULL MOON / WANING

GOALS THIS WEEK:

REMINDER:

TO-DO LIST:

# Weekly Schedule

## September

**5**
MON

........................................................................

**6**
TUE

........................................................................

**7**
WED

........................................................................

**8**
THURS

........................................................................

**9**
FRI

........................................................................

**10**
SAT

........................................................................

**11**
SUN

........................................................................

# Weekly Planner

MOON PHASE:   NEW MOON / WAXING / FULL MOON / WANING

GOALS THIS WEEK:

REMINDER:

TO-DO LIST:

# Weekly Schedule

## September

**12**
MON

.......................................................................................

**13**
TUE

.......................................................................................

**14**
WED

.......................................................................................

**15**
THURS

.......................................................................................

**16**
FRI

.......................................................................................

**17**
SAT

.......................................................................................

**18**
SUN

.......................................................................................

# Weekly Planner

MOON PHASE:   NEW MOON / WAXING / FULL MOON / WANING

GOALS THIS WEEK:

REMINDER:

TO-DO LIST:

# Weekly Schedule

## September

19
MON
....................................................................................

20
TUE
....................................................................................

21
WED
....................................................................................

22
THURS
....................................................................................

23
FRI
....................................................................................

24
SAT
....................................................................................

25
SUN
....................................................................................

# Weekly Planner

MOON PHASE:  NEW MOON / WAXING / FULL MOON / WANING

GOALS THIS WEEK:

REMINDER:

TO-DO LIST:

# Weekly Schedule

## September - October

26 ●
MON
................................................................................

27
TUE
................................................................................

28
WED
................................................................................

29
THURS
................................................................................

30
FRI
................................................................................

1
SAT
................................................................................

2
SUN
................................................................................

# Seasonal Review

# October

**KEY FOCUS FOR THIS MONTH:**

| MON | TUE | WED | THUR | FRI | SAT | SUN |
|-----|-----|-----|------|-----|-----|-----|
|  |  |  |  |  | 1 | 2 |
| 3 | 4 | 5 | 6 | 7 | 8 | 9 |
| 10 ☽ ♈ 11 | 12 | 13 | 14 | 15 | 16 | |
| 17 | 18 | 19 | 20 | 21 | 22 | 23 |
| 24 | 25 ● ♏ 26 | 27 | 28 | 29 | 30 | |

♈ FULL MOON IN ARIES          ♏ NEW MOON ECLIPSE
IN SCORPIO

# GOALS THIS MONTH:

# Weekly Planner

**MOON PHASE:** NEW MOON / WAXING / FULL MOON / WANING

### GOALS THIS WEEK:

### REMINDER:

### TO-DO LIST:

# Weekly Schedule

## October

3
MON

4
TUE

5
WED

6
THURS

7
FRI

8
SAT

9
SUN

# Weekly Planner

## GOALS THIS WEEK:

## REMINDER:

## TO-DO LIST:

# Weekly Schedule

## October

10
MON

....................................................................

11
TUE

....................................................................

12
WED

....................................................................

13
THURS

....................................................................

14
FRI

....................................................................

15
SAT

....................................................................

16
SUN

....................................................................

# Weekly Planner

GOALS THIS WEEK:

REMINDER:

TO-DO LIST:

# Weekly Schedule

## October

**17**
MON

**18**
TUE

**19**
WED

**20**
THURS

**21**
FRI

**22**
SAT

**23**
SUN

# Weekly Planner

GOALS THIS WEEK:

REMINDER:

TO-DO LIST:

# Weekly Schedule

## October

24
MON

............................................

25 ●
TUE

............................................

26
WED

............................................

27
THURS

............................................

28
FRI

............................................

29
SAT

............................................

30
SUN

............................................

# November

**KEY FOCUS FOR THIS MONTH:**

*It's time to order next year's planner!*

| MON | TUE | WED | THUR | FRI | SAT | SUN |
|-----|-----|-----|------|-----|-----|-----|
| 31 | 1 | 2 | 3 | 4 | 5 | 6 |
| 7 | 8 ☽ ♉ 9 | | 10 | 11 | 12 | 13 |
| 14 | 15 | 16 | 17 | 18 | 19 | 20 |
| 21 | 22 | 23 | 24 ● ♐ 25 | | 26 | 27 |
| 28 | 29 | 30 | | | | |

♉ FULL MOON ECLIPSE IN TAURUS    ♐ NEW MOON IN SAGITTARIUS

# GOALS THIS MONTH:

# Weekly Planner

MOON PHASE:  NEW MOON / WAXING / FULL MOON / WANING

GOALS THIS WEEK:

REMINDER:

TO-DO LIST:

# Weekly Schedule

## October - November

31
MON

........................................................

1
TUE

........................................................

2
WED

........................................................

3
THURS

........................................................

4
FRI

........................................................

5
SAT

........................................................

6
SUN

........................................................

# Weekly Planner

MOON PHASE:  NEW MOON / WAXING / FULL MOON / WANING

GOALS THIS WEEK:

REMINDER:

TO-DO LIST:

# Weekly Schedule

## November

**7**
MON
....................................................................................

**8**
TUE
....................................................................................

**9**
WED
....................................................................................

**10**
THURS
....................................................................................

**11**
FRI
....................................................................................

**12**
SAT
....................................................................................

**13**
SUN
....................................................................................

# Weekly Planner

MOON PHASE:  NEW MOON / WAXING / FULL MOON / WANING

GOALS THIS WEEK:

REMINDER:

TO-DO LIST:

# Weekly Schedule

## November

14
MON

................................................................

15
TUE

................................................................

16
WED

................................................................

17
THURS

................................................................

18
FRI

................................................................

19
SAT

................................................................

20
SUN

................................................................

# Weekly Planner

**MOON PHASE:** NEW MOON / WAXING / FULL MOON / WANING

**GOALS THIS WEEK:**

**REMINDER:**

**TO-DO LIST:**

# Weekly Schedule

## November

21
MON

.................................................................

22
TUE

.................................................................

23
WED

.................................................................

24 ●
THURS

.................................................................

25
FRI

.................................................................

26
SAT

.................................................................

27
SUN

.................................................................

# December

KEY FOCUS FOR THIS MONTH:

| MON | TUE | WED | THUR | FRI | SAT | SUN |
|---|---|---|---|---|---|---|
| | | | 1 | 2 | 3 | 4 |
| 5 | 6 | 7 | 8 ♊ | 9 | 10 | 11 |
| 12 | 13 | 14 | 15 | 16 | 17 | 18 |
| 19 | 20 | 21 | 22 | 23 ♑ | 24 | 25 |
| 26 | 27 | 28 | 29 | 30 | 31 | |

♊ Full moon in Gemini    ♑ Super New moon in Capricorn

# GOALS THIS MONTH:

# Weekly Planner

MOON PHASE:  NEW MOON / WAXING / FULL MOON / WANING

GOALS THIS WEEK:

REMINDER:

TO-DO LIST:

# Weekly Schedule

## November - December

**28**
MON
.................................................................

**29**
TUE
.................................................................

**30**
WED
.................................................................

**1**
THURS
.................................................................

**2**
FRI
.................................................................

**3**
SAT
.................................................................

**4**
SUN
.................................................................

# Weekly Planner

MOON PHASE: NEW MOON / WAXING / FULL MOON / WANING

GOALS THIS WEEK:

REMINDER:

TO-DO LIST:

# Weekly Schedule

## December

5
MON

6
TUE

7
WED

8
THURS

9
FRI

10
SAT

11
SUN

# Weekly Planner

MOON PHASE:  NEW MOON / WAXING / FULL MOON / WANING

GOALS THIS WEEK:

REMINDER:

TO-DO LIST:

# Weekly Schedule

## December

12
MON

--------------------------------------------------

13
TUE

--------------------------------------------------

14
WED

--------------------------------------------------

15
THURS

--------------------------------------------------

16
FRI

--------------------------------------------------

17
SAT

--------------------------------------------------

18
SUN

--------------------------------------------------

# Weekly Planner

GOALS THIS WEEK:

REMINDER:

TO-DO LIST:

# Weekly Schedule

## December

19
MON

20
TUE

21
WED

22
THURS

23 ●
FRI

24
SAT

25
SUN

# Weekly Planner

GOALS THIS WEEK:

REMINDER:

TO-DO LIST:

# Weekly Schedule

## December - January

26
MON
..................................................................

27
TUE
..................................................................

28
WED
..................................................................

29
THURS
..................................................................

30
FRI
..................................................................

31
SAT
..................................................................

1
SUN
..................................................................

# Seasonal
# Review

*A flower blossoms*
*for its own joy*

*- Oscar Wilde*

You can order next year's planner, books and other products at:
www.SzeWingVetault.com

# About Sze Wing Vetault

Sze Wing is a coach, author and creative entrepreneur. She works with career women, busy mums and purpose-driven business owners to become goddesses in all aspects of their lives. She helps women to uncover their feminine wisdom to find better work-life balance, more joy, and sustainable success in life.

With a background in Economics (BSc.) and Political Sciences (MSc.), she has built a diverse career as a business consultant for private and public companies in education and media.

Sze Wing runs a blog & podcast, and she teaches experiential workshops both online and in-person. She works with entrepreneurs to publish their non-fiction books and other creative products. She is also a mum to two beautiful young children.

She loves yoga, dance and travel with her family. Her favourite morning ritual includes mediation, journaling, and sipping a good cuppa!

For more information, please visit her website at:
www.SzeWingVetault.com

2022